Understanding the Bible

Loveland, Colorado

Group's R.E.A.L. Guarantee to you:

This Group resource incorporates our R.E.A.L. approach to ministry—one that encourages long-term retention and life transformation. It's ministry that's:

Relational

Because learner-to-learner interaction enhances learning and builds Christian friendships.

Experiential

Because what learners experience through discussion and action sticks with them up to 9 times longer than what they simply hear or read.

Applicable

Because the aim of Christian education is to equip learners to be both hearers and doers of God's Word.

Learner-based

Because learners understand and retain more when the learning process takes into consideration how they learn best.

Understanding the Bible

Junior High Bible Study Series

Copyright © 2003 Group Publishing, Inc.

Visit our Web site: **www.grouppublishing.com**

Credits
Contributing Authors: Lisa Baba Lauffer, Stephen Parolini, James Selman, and Michael D. Warden
Editor: Kelli B. Trujillo
Creative Development Editor: Amy Simpson
Chief Creative Officer: Joani Schultz
Copy Editor: Deirdre Brouer
Art Director: Sharon Anderson
Cover Art Director: Jeff A. Storm
Photographer: Daniel Treat
Print Production Artist: Tracy K. Donaldson
Illustrator: Matt Wood
Production Manager: DeAnne Lear

ISBN 0-7644-2461-0
10 9 8 7 6 5 4 3 2   12 11 10 09 08 07 06 05 04 03

Printed in the United States of America.

Table of Contents

Understanding the Bible

Today's young people are facing major crises concerning both who they are and who they can trust. They face decisions about friendship and dating. They face discouragement and loneliness. They encounter divorce, drugs, and drinking. They live in a world that is constantly changing—a world that can be pretty scary.

How can teenagers navigate through this jungle of choices, temptations, and roller-coaster emotions?

With God's Word as their compass. Through the Bible, teenagers can not only learn to distinguish right from wrong but also discover who God is in a deeply personal way. They can discover God's love and realize that God desires to live in relationship with them.

But first they need to know where to start. After all, a compass won't do much good if someone doesn't know how to use it, right? Faith 4 Life: Junior High Bible Study Series, *Understanding the Bible* will give your students a basic overview of what the Bible is, how it all fits together, and how to use the Bible to traverse life's tough choices.

In the first study, teenagers will discover how incredible the Bible is by looking more closely at how it was written. They'll be challenged to make reading the Bible a top priority.

Next your students will examine the relationship between the laws of the Old Testament and Jesus' teachings in the New Testament. Teenagers will learn that Jesus is the fulfillment of the Old Testament laws. They'll be inspired to apply Jesus' teaching from the Sermon on the Mount to their lives.

In the third study, teenagers will examine some of the "gray" areas of Scripture and will seek basic principles they can use to find guidance from God's Word, even regarding issues that the Bible doesn't directly address.

The last study will help students learn that studying the Bible and applying what they learn to the choices they make can dramatically change their lives. They'll be encouraged as they consider how God's Word can empower them to grow by leaps and bounds in their faith.

When your teenagers understand that the Bible can speak directly to them and can relate to their daily lives and all the issues they encounter, they'll be equipped with the ultimate road map through all the traps, trials, and temptations of the junior high jungle.

Through the Bible, teenagers can not only learn to distinguish right from wrong but also discover who God is in a deeply personal way.

About Faith 4 Life

Use Faith 4 Life studies to show your teenagers how the Bible is relevant to their lives. Help them see that God can invade every area of their lives and change them in ways they can only imagine. Encourage your students to go deeper into faith—faith that will sustain them for life! Faith 4 Life, forever!

Faith 4 Life: Junior High Bible Study Series helps young teenagers take a Bible-based approach to faith and life issues. Each book in the series contains these important elements:

■ **Life application of Bible truth**—Faith 4 Life studies help teenagers understand what the Bible says, then apply that truth to their lives.

■ **A relevant topic**—Each Faith 4 Life book focuses on one main topic, with four studies to give your students a thorough understanding of how the Bible relates to that topic. Youth leaders chose these topics as the ones most relevant for junior high students.

■ **One point**—Each study makes one point, centering on that one theme to make sure students really understand the important truth it conveys. This point is stated upfront and throughout the study.

■ **Simplicity**—The studies are easy to use. Each contains a "Before the Study" box that outlines any advance preparation required. Each study also contains a "Study at a Glance" chart so you can quickly and easily see what supplies you'll need and what each study will involve.

■ **Action and interaction**—Each study relies on experiential learning to help students learn what God's Word has to say. Teenagers discuss and debrief their experiences in large groups, small groups, and individual reflection.

■ **Reproducible handouts**—Faith 4 Life books include reproducible handouts for students. No need for student books!

■ **Tips, tips, and more tips**—Faith 4 Life studies are full of "FYI" tips for the teacher that provide extra ideas, insights into young people, and hints for making the studies go smoothly.

■ **Flexibility**—Faith 4 Life studies include optional activities and bonus activities. Use a study as it's written, or use these options to create the study that works best for your group.

■ **Follow-up Ideas**—At the end of each book, you'll find a section called "Changed 4 Life." This section provides ideas for following up with your students to make sure the studies stick with them.

The Making of the Bible

ANCIENT

SALVATION

RELEVANT

hope

The Bible...

...was written in three languages—Hebrew, Aramaic, and Greek!

...includes history, prayers, worship songs, poems, prophecies, and letters!

...was written by more than forty people, yet maintains one consistent theme—God's redemption of humankind!

...is available in more than 2,000 languages!

...was written on three continents—Asia, Africa, and Europe!

...was written over the course of 1,600 years and sixty generations!

...is the best-selling book in world history!

How many of the teenagers in your youth ministry know all this great stuff about the Bible? Do they think it's just an old book of fables and fairy tales, or do they understand its power to revolutionize their lives?

This study delves into the incredible way God created the Bible and will whet your students' appetites for reading the Bible and applying it to their lives. Through this exploration, teenagers will discover the miracle of how the Bible was created and will begin to see how God's Word applies to them today.

The Point

▶ The Bible is the most incredible book you could ever read.

Scripture Source

Romans 15:4

Paul writes about the purpose of Scripture.

2 Timothy 3:16-17

Paul writes about the usefulness of Scripture.

Hebrews 4:12

The writer compares God's Word to a double-edged sword.

2 Peter 1:20-21

Peter explains that God, through the Holy Spirit, inspired people to write the Bible.

The Study at a Glance

Warm-Up (20-25 minutes)

Tell Me a Story

What students will do: Create a giant book that describes the most incredible books they can imagine.

Needs: ❑ Bibles ❑ duct tape
❑ scissors ❑ markers
❑ paper ❑ newsprint
❑ two cardboard boxes
❑ masking tape
❑ construction paper

Bible Connection (20-25 minutes)

The Big Picture

What students will do: Create a giant puzzle that forms a unified picture of the Bible's creation.

Needs: ❑ Bibles ❑ scissors
❑ markers ❑ duct tape
❑ masking tape ❑ newsprint
❑ "The Most Incredible Book in the World" handouts (p. 17)

Life Application (5-10 minutes)

Checking It Out

What students will do: Explore a Scripture passage to gain new insights.

Needs: ❑ Bibles ❑ paper
❑ pencils ❑ duct tape
❑ masking tape ❑ newsprint

Bonus Activity (5-10 minutes)

What students will do: Form Bible Study Partnerships and commit to a Bible study plan for the upcoming week.

Needs: ❑ "B.S.P." handouts (p. 18)
❑ pens or pencils

Before the Study →

Find two medium-sized cardboard boxes for the Warm-Up activity. Each box should be approximately the size of a small microwave oven. Also collect several pairs of scissors, some duct tape, markers, newsprint, and enough construction paper so that each student can have one or two pieces. Set these supplies out on a table, or place them in another easily accessible area of the room.

For "The Big Picture" activity, make one copy of "The Most Incredible Book in the World" handout (p. 17) for every fourteen teenagers in your group. Cut along the dotted lines on the handouts to create strips. Take some time to create a puzzle by ripping a sheet of newsprint into enough pieces so that each pair of teenagers will have one piece.

If you choose to do the Bonus Activity, you'll need to make one copy of the "B.S.P." handout (p. 18) for each student.

Warm-Up

Tell Me a Story
(20 to 25 minutes)

As teenagers arrive, have them form pairs.

SAY:

■ Tell your partner the name of your favorite book and why you like it.

After pairs exchange this information,

SAY:

■ Tell your partner one way he or she reminds you of a positive character in your book.

When they've finished,

SAY:

■ There are so many types of books available for us to read, such as fantasy, science fiction, and biographies. We have so much to choose from! Today we're going to explore the most incredible book you could ever read. To begin our exploration, we're going to create our own book.

Give the group two medium-sized cardboard boxes. Have students collapse the boxes and cut each box along one of its folds. Lay the boxes side by side on the floor. Duct tape the touching edges together down the length of the cardboard. Flip the boxes over, and tape the seam again. Then stand the "book" on its end in the center of the room.

Give each student a sheet of construction paper and a marker.

SAY:

■ Imagine the most incredible book that could ever be written. Think about the topic of the book, what kinds of information or stories it would include, and what kind of power it would have to change lives.

Give students a few seconds to do this, then

SAY:

■ I'm going to ask you some questions about the incredible book that you've imagined. Write your answers on your sheet of construction paper.

ASK:

■ Where did this book come from?
■ Who wrote this book?
■ Why is this book so incredible?
■ What message does this book have for you?

After teenagers write their answers, instruct them to tape the construction paper to the outside of the front and back covers of your giant cardboard book. Have the group brainstorm a title for the book, such as "The Biggest and Best Book in the World." Write the title on construction paper, and tape it to the front cover.

Have teenagers form pairs, and

ASK:

■ What would make a book seem incredible to you?

Have each person write his or her partner's response on a sheet of paper. Have teenagers read what their partners wrote. Then have pairs answer these questions:

■ How well did your partner express what you said?
■ What was it like to have someone else write your thoughts for you?

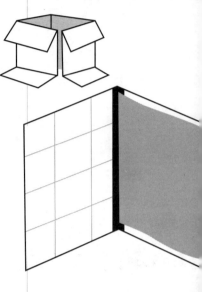

FYI

If you have more than fifty students, consider creating more than one book.

FYI

The covers of your book may sag if the cardboard and duct tape are too weak. To avoid this, lean the book in a corner of your meeting room or along a wall.

If you lean your book in a corner or along a wall, have teenagers tape the construction paper to the inside of the book covers for easier access.

■ If someone were writing your life story, how would you make sure he or she got the story right?

■ Who would you trust to write your life story? Why?

FYI Prevent the newsprint pages from sagging by clipping them to the book covers with jumbo paper clips.

Have teenagers tape their partners' responses to a sheet of newsprint. Set the left edge of the newsprint next to the inside seam of the book cover. Duct tape the newsprint into the binding of the cover.

SAY:

■ Just as we had other people writing our responses for us, God used other people to write his Word to us.

Distribute Bibles, and invite a teenager to read aloud 2 Peter 1:20-21.

SAY:

The Point ▶ ■ This is one of the reasons why <u>the Bible is the most incredible book you could ever read.</u> As we create the next pages of our book, we're going to learn even more about how God created his incredible book.

Bible Connection

The Big Picture
(20 to 25 minutes)

SAY:

■ Before we begin exploring the creation of the Bible, let's pray that God would teach us about his Word.

PRAY:

■ Dear God, we want to know more about the book you wrote for us. As we explore it today, please help us learn what you want us to know. Amen.

SAY:

■ We're going to create a page for our book that describes the way God wrote the Bible. As you work, think of how creating this page is like or unlike the way God created the Bible.

Have teenagers form pairs. Give each pair one piece of the ripped newsprint, a marker, and one or more sections of the "Most Incredible Book in the World" handout (p. 17). If you have more than seven pairs, make several copies of the handout, and give some pairs duplicate sections.

SAY:

■ Read your Bible fact, then work with your partner to draw on your piece of newsprint a symbol that represents what you learned.

When pairs finish drawing, have them explain their symbols and put the puzzle pieces of newsprint together on top of another sheet of newsprint. Have pairs tape the pieces together as they go. Then have the group duct tape the page into the book.

Have pairs discuss these questions:

■ What does this page of our book tell us about the Bible?
■ How was creating this page similar to how God created the Bible? How was it different?
■ How does learning about how God created the Bible change what you think of it?

Have pairs read 2 Timothy 3:16-17 and discuss these questions:

■ What do these verses say to you about the Bible?
■ Do you struggle with reading the Bible regularly? Why or why not?
■ Based on today's study, will you change how much you read the Bible? Why or why not?

SAY:

■ <u>The Bible is the most incredible book you could ever read.</u> ◀ **The Point**
God created it in such a unique way, with many people from different places contributing to it over a long period of time. Yet like our puzzle, it communicates one unified message: God loves and forgives us. Because the Bible is so incredible, we can learn so much when we read it.

Checking It Out
(5 to 10 minutes)

Have teenagers form trios. Give each trio paper and a pencil. Have each trio choose a scribe to write the trio's responses, an encourager to keep everyone involved in the discussion, and a reporter to present the trio's insights to the group.

SAY:

■ We're going to have a little contest. I'm going to give you a Scripture verse to read, and you have three minutes to write as many insights from that verse as you can. For example, one of your insights might be, "The Bible is a living book."

Have trios read Hebrews 4:12 and write their insights. After three minutes, have reporters share how many insights their trios thought of and what those insights are. Make sure each trio shares at least one insight.

Give each student two sheets of paper and a pencil.

SAY:

■ Think of one way this verse can apply to your life in the coming week.

Direct students to write their answers on a sheet of paper and to tape their papers to one sheet of newsprint. Duct tape the newsprint into the book.

SAY:

■ <u>The Bible is the most incredible book you could ever read.</u> ◀ **The Point** Based on what you've learned today, make a commitment about reading the Bible this week. For example, you might commit to read a chapter every morning before you go to school. When you've thought of your commitment, write it on another piece of paper, and sign your name.

Before teenagers leave, have them tape their papers to newsprint. Duct tape the newsprint into the book, and then close the study in a group prayer.

(5 to 10 minutes)

If you have time, try this activity before you wrap up the study. Have teenagers form pairs, and distribute a copy of the "B.S.P." handout (p. 18) to each student. Explain that teenagers should work in their pairs to look at the list of topics on the handout and pick five topics they are both interested in learning more about. Challenge the students to commit to a "Bible Study Partnership" for the next week. Prompt them to use the handout to plan which topic they'll study each day for the next five days and to make arrangements to call or e-mail each other daily to give each other updates on what they learned.

The Most Incredible Book in the World

The Bible was written over the course of 1,600 years and sixty generations.

God wrote the Bible through more than forty people. Some of these people were kings, fishermen, scholars, and peasants.

God, through the Holy Spirit, directed some authors to write his message immediately and allowed others to share his message orally through the generations.

The Bible was written on three continents—Asia, Africa, and Europe—and in many different types of places such as prisons, palaces, in the wilderness, and on the road.

The Bible was written in three languages: Hebrew, Aramaic, and Greek.

The Bible includes history, prayers, worship songs, poems, prophecies, and letters.

Biblical authors wrote about many controversial subjects yet maintained one consistent theme: God loves us and forgives us for our sins.

B.S.P.

It's official. You and your partner have now formed a B.S.P. (Bible Study Partnership). You'll work together this next week to discover what the Bible says about some topics that interest you.

Look at the list below, and circle five topics that you both are interested in reading more about.

- friends (Proverbs 17:17; 18:24)
- enemies (Matthew 5:43-47)
- hard times (Romans 5:3-5; James 1:2-4)
- parents (Ephesians 6:1-4)
- drugs and alcohol (Ephesians 5:18)
- peer pressure (Romans 12:2)

- worry (Matthew 6:25-34; Philippians 4:6-9)
- busyness (Psalm 46:10)
- forgiveness (Colossians 3:13)
- prayer (Matthew 6:5-13)
- love (1 Corinthians 13:4-7)
- temptation (1 Corinthians 10:13)

Next decide which topic you'd like to study each day, and write the day of the week next to each topic you circled.

Now make your plans. Basically what you'll do is read the Scripture(s) listed by the topic for each day, take notes on any observations or important points you discover, and then call or e-mail your partner to talk about what you've learned. Use the questions below to guide your study, and make sure to write down your partner's e-mail address or phone number.

Questions to Consider

- **Who is talking or writing?**
- **What words or phrases stand out to you?**
- **What appears to be the main point?**
- **How does this apply to your own life?**

Bible Study Partner's e-mail/phone number: _____

A New Look at the Old Law

love

rules

"**L**ook both ways before you cross the street."

"Say, 'please.' "

"Do your homework before you watch TV."

Rules. Young teenagers know all about them. They've had to live under them since the day they were born. There are rules at home, rules at school, rules at the mall, and, yes, even rules at church. And when some teenagers think of the Bible, guess what comes to mind? That's right—more rules.

This Bible study will help teenagers understand some basics about the laws in the Old Testament that governed the lives of God's people and will help them see how Jesus' teachings in the New Testament sheds light on those Old Testament laws. This study will help students discover some of Jesus' most central teachings from the Sermon on the Mount and will challenge them to apply those principles to their lives.

The Point

▶ Jesus' teachings provide a new perspective on Old Testament laws.

Scripture Source

Jeremiah 31:31-34

Jeremiah writes of a time God will make a new covenant with his people.

Matthew 5:17-48

Jesus describes how he came to fulfill Old Testament laws and prophecies.

The Study at a Glance

Warm-Up (up to 15 minutes)

The Perfect Society

What students will do: Create fictional countries and determine their countries' rules.

Needs: ❑ newsprint
❑ markers

Optional Activity (up to 15 minutes)

What students will do: Try to follow rules for an activity and get penalized for every rule they break.

Needs: ❑ paper
❑ tape
❑ self-stick notes

Bible Connection (20-30 minutes)

A New Understanding

What students will do: Discover how Jesus brought new perspectives to Old Testament laws.

Needs: ❑ Bibles
❑ "Old Laws, New Perspectives" handouts (p. 28)
❑ marker
❑ newsprint
❑ tape
❑ white paper

Life Application (10-15 minutes)

New Perspectives

What students will do: Commit to follow Jesus' teachings.

Needs: ❑ "Old Laws, New Perspectives" handouts (p. 28)
❑ pens or pencils

Before the Study

Make enough photocopies of the "Old Laws, New Perspectives" handout (p. 28) so that each student can have one. Make sure the copies are made on white paper—the thinner the paper, the better.

Warm-Up

The Perfect Society
(up to 15 minutes)

Begin by having teenagers form groups of no more than five. Give each group a sheet of newsprint and a marker.

SAY:

- For the next few minutes, your group will be a brand new country. You've each decided to start a new society that will not have all the problems you see in the world around you.
- In your group, first decide the name of your country and where it will be located. Write this information on your newsprint. Then take a few minutes to decide on the laws of your country in order to keep it safe, happy, and free from negative influences such as crime, drugs, and violence.
- Write each law you agree upon on your newsprint. Also make sure to discuss and write down the punishments for breaking the laws.

After five to seven minutes, have groups present their countries and laws to the rest of the students. Have teenagers ask questions about other groups' laws if they don't agree with them or if they need clarification. Point out any similarities between the laws that groups create. Then

ASK:

- How easy was it to create laws for your country? Explain.
- Would it be easy to enforce the laws you created? Why or why not?
- Do you think any of the punishments we've discussed seem too harsh? Do any of them seem too light?
- Could you stop people from thinking about breaking the laws? Explain.

FYI Allow teenagers to think of silly laws and punishments such as "All citizens must eat chocolate for breakfast every day" or "Breaking this law results in being forced to watch reruns of TV shows from the '80s for five full days." However, encourage groups to also focus on some serious rules and punishments that they believe are essential to help their society run smoothly.

SAY:

■ Jesus surprised many people when he taught the disciples about the well-established Old Testament laws. Instead of simply restating what people already knew, Jesus taught that people's thoughts and motives for their actions are as important as their actions. In this lesson we'll see that <u>Jesus' teach-</u> ◀ **The Point** <u>ings provide a new perspective on Old Testament laws,</u> and we'll explore how this new way of thinking applies to us today.

★ Optional Activity

(up to 15 minutes)

Instead of having teenagers make laws for a perfect society, try this activity. Have teenagers form groups of three or four. Give each group a supply of paper and tape. Then

SAY:

■ **I'm going to give you very specific rules for an activity. You must follow my rules exactly or your group will be penalized by receiving a self-stick note. Each self-stick note represents one time your group broke a rule.**

Give the following instructions, pausing to allow groups to complete them. If you see a group not following through exactly as you've instructed, penalize it by placing a self-stick note on someone in that group. Watch closely, and look for any small mistakes groups might make.

<u>Instructions:</u>

1. **Have each person in your group roll up three pieces of paper into cylinders and tape them so they won't unroll. You may not speak at all during this activity.** Penalize groups that talk or roll up the wrong number of cylinders.

2. **Stand the cylinders in a circle on the floor, and tape them together to create a large circle that will serve as a base for your tower. You must all be talking during this activity until I say "stop."** Penalize groups that have quiet group members or that don't create the right kind of base as indicated in the picture (on p. 23). Call out "stop" before reading the next instruction.

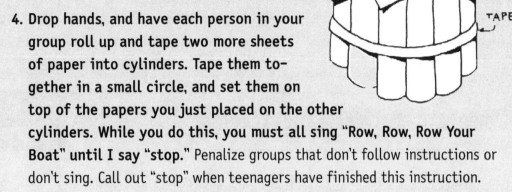

3. **Hold hands in your group, and work together to lay four sheets of paper on the top of the cylinder base without letting go of one another's hands.** Penalize groups that don't hold hands or that use the wrong number of sheets of paper.

4. **Drop hands, and have each person in your group roll up and tape two more sheets of paper into cylinders. Tape them together in a small circle, and set them on top of the papers you just placed on the other cylinders. While you do this, you must all sing "Row, Row, Row Your Boat" until I say "stop."** Penalize groups that don't follow instructions or don't sing. Call out "stop" when teenagers have finished this instruction.

5. **Now jump up and down three times, spin in place once, do four jumping jacks, nod your head twice, and shake hands with someone who isn't in a different group.** Watch closely here—you should be able to give out lots of self-stick notes.

Ask teenagers to look around at the other groups, noting the number of self-stick notes each has.

SAY:
■ Each self-stick note represents one time someone in your group didn't follow the rules exactly.

While teenagers are still in their groups,

ASK:
■ How do you feel about being penalized for making even the smallest mistake?
■ How did you feel as you tried to exactly follow every rule?
■ How might this be similar to the way the people in Jesus' time felt as they tried to follow every Old Testament law?
■ How is following these rules like following the rules we have in life?

SAY:
■ The people of Jesus' time had many rules to follow too. But when Jesus taught about the rules, he added a new dimension to the people's understanding. <u>Jesus' teachings provide a new perspective on Old Testament laws.</u> Let's explore that dimension by having you follow

The Point ▶

one final rule in your group. Here's the rule: If you ever even thought once of not obeying one of these rules or that they were stupid, you must tear down your tower.

Allow time for teenagers to tear down the towers. Then

SAY:

■ Our thoughts and feelings are just as important as following all the rules. Jesus taught this new idea in his Sermon on the Mount—and it's still true today.

A New Understanding
(20 to 30 minutes)

Bible Connection

Invite students to form trios, and tell them they have just three minutes to scan through their Bibles for examples of some Old Testament laws. Tell them to try and find a law or rule that they hadn't heard of before or one that seems unusual or extremely specific. This means that most of them should probably find something other than the Ten Commandments. Direct students to focus on Exodus, Leviticus, and Deuteronomy. When time is up, give trios a moment to quickly explain the law or rule they discovered.

ASK:

■ Are these the kinds of laws you expected to find? Why or why not?

■ What do you think the purposes were for these laws?

SAY:

■ Perhaps the most notable set of laws in the Old Testament is the Ten Commandments.

ASK:

■ Can you name any of the Ten Commandments? (If students need help, point them to Exodus 20:1-17.)

■ What do you think the purposes were for these laws?

■ Can you think of modern laws that are based on these Old Testament laws? What are they?

FYI

Warning! Some of the laws in the Old Testament deal with issues related to sexuality and personal cleanliness. If teenagers select one of these laws as the example they'd like to share, encourage them to try to find something else that's more appropriate for group discussion.

SAY:

■ The Old Testament contains laws that governed the lives of God's people. The laws provided guidelines for worshipping God, making moral decisions, respecting others, and even eating healthy foods and avoiding disease.

Have a volunteer read aloud Jeremiah 31:31-34.

SAY:

■ Even before Jesus came on the scene, the prophet Jeremiah prophesied about a time the Law would be written upon people's hearts—when people would understand the reason for the Law and would live it in both thought and action.

Give each teenager a copy of the "Old Laws, New Perspectives" handout (p. 28).

SAY:

■ A few Old Testament laws, similar to the ones we've discussed, are listed on the left side of your handout. (Allow students a moment to read these laws.) They're important laws. But Jesus' Sermon on the Mount added a new perspective to the laws. Fold your paper in half, and hold it up to a light to see the new perspectives Jesus brought to the laws.

Teenagers should be able to read the backward writing once the handout has been folded. Allow a minute or two for teenagers to read the handout. (To see how this works, check out the illustration in the margin.)

Have teenagers form groups of no more than four, and have volunteers in each group read aloud Matthew 5:17-48. While they're reading, list the following questions on a sheet of newsprint, and tape it on the wall so teenagers can see it.

The Point ▶ ■ How do <u>Jesus' teachings in this passage provide a new perspective on Old Testament laws?</u>

■ Does it seem like Jesus is changing any of the laws, or is he just explaining them? Defend your answer.

■ What do you think Jesus meant when he said he was a fulfillment of the Law and the Prophets?

■ How do you think the people felt when they heard Jesus' message in this passage?

■ Why was Jesus' message so strong?

■ What general principles can we learn from this Scripture passage?

Have groups discuss the questions for a few minutes. Then gather together, and have groups each share one thing they learned from their discussion time.

SAY:

- If we took Jesus' message literally, we probably wouldn't have many eyes or hands left. But Jesus didn't intend to make more rules; instead he intended for people to live—as Jeremiah prophesied—with the Law in their hearts so it would guide not only their actions but also their thoughts.

New Perspectives
(10 to 15 minutes)

SAY:

- Hold up your "Old Laws, New Perspectives" handout to a light again, and think of ways you can follow each new perspective in your own life. Write your thoughts next to each New Perspective on your handout. For example, you might write, "I will try not to get angry with my brother when he borrows stuff from me." Make your commitments as specific as possible. Then sign your name across the top of your handout as a commitment to follow Jesus' teachings.

Have teenagers form groups of no more than four and share one way they decided to follow Jesus' teachings.

After a few minutes,

SAY:

- Jesus' message in Matthew 5:17-48 gives us a new perspective on Old Testament laws—he reminds us that we need to seek a life that's pleasing to God in both action and thought. The nice surprise is that if we commit to following Jesus' teachings in our hearts, we'll naturally follow his teachings and the Old Testament commandments with our actions.

◀ **The Point**

Invite teenagers to form groups of no more than three.

SAY:

- Jesus loved us enough to teach us how to live according to God's ways. In your group, think of a way you can express

FYI

Believe it or not, this creative way of saying "thanks" to Jesus is a form of prayer! It's a hands-on, one-of-a-kind way for your students to express their thankfulness to God. As you wrap up this closing activity, explain to students that they've just prayed in a nonconventional way. Use this as a starting point to encourage other forms of prayer and worship that involve activity, sight, smell, and sound.

your thanks to Jesus for teaching us how to live. You might choose to create a short cheer or to form yourselves into a human sculpture representing your thankfulness.

Allow a couple of minutes for groups to choose what they'll do. Then have groups simultaneously offer their thanks to Jesus in their creative ways. Afterward, tell groups how much you enjoyed each creative expression. Encourage teenagers to share what they like most about one another's thankful expressions before they leave the study.

Old Laws, New Perspectives

Old Laws

DO NOT MURDER...

DO NOT COMMIT ADULTERY...

EYE FOR EYE, AND TOOTH FOR TOOTH...

LOVE YOUR NEIGHBOR AND HATE YOUR ENEMY...

New Perspectives

"You have heard that it was said
to the people long ago,

But I tell you that anyone who is angry
with his brother will be subject to judgment.".

"You have heard that it was said,

But I tell you that anyone who looks at a
woman lustfully has already committed
adultery with her in his heart.".

"You have heard that it was said,

But I tell you, Do not resist an evil person.
If someone strikes you on the right cheek,
turn to him the other also.".

"You have heard that it was said,

But I tell you: Love your enemies and
pray for those who persecute you.".
(Matthew 5:21-22, 27-28, 38-39, 43-44)

Gray Areas?

BIBLE

QUESTIONS

direction?

How far is too far to go physically in a dating relationship?

What's wrong with taking just one sip of beer or smoking just one cigarette?

If taking drugs is wrong, why doesn't the Bible ever directly condemn it?

These questions can be sizzling discussion starters for your youth group. But they're also all related to one whopper of a question that has plagued churches (and youth groups) for hundreds of years: Why does the Bible seem vague about some issues?

This study challenges young people to confront these vague issues and discover how God's Word can still provide teenagers with a powerful guide for life, even when the answers aren't spelled out in black and white.

The Point

▶ The Bible is your guide for life.

Scripture Source

Romans 14:4-19

Paul instructs us not to judge other Christians.

1 Corinthians 6:12-20

Paul warns us to avoid sexual immorality.

1 Corinthians 10:23-33

Paul encourages us not to let our freedom cause others to stumble.

Ephesians 5:15-18

Paul tells us not to get drunk but to be filled with God's Spirit.

1 John 2:27-29

John explains how God's Spirit teaches us what is right.

The Study at a Glance

Warm-Up (10-15 minutes)

Whaddya Think?

What students will do: Form groups to discuss controversial opinions about the Bible.

Needs: ❏ "The Bible—Can You Trust It?" handouts (p. 36)

Optional Activity (10-15 minutes)

What students will do: Survey their peers about their opinions of the Bible and present their findings.

Needs: ❏ paper
❏ pens or pencils
❏ markers
❏ "Pollsters!" handouts (pp. 37-38)

Bible Connection (20-25 minutes)

Three Shades of Gray

What students will do: Work with partners to create symbols of three issues that aren't clearly wrong or right and search Scripture to find answers.

Needs: ❏ Bibles
❏ three tables
❏ newsprint
❏ tape
❏ markers
❏ white paper
❏ construction paper

Life Application (15-20 minutes)

Gray Fusion

What students will do: Combine their symbols into one unique sculpture and discuss how accepting gray areas of truth can help them understand God and the Bible.

Needs: ❏ tape   ❏ string

Before the Study ➡

For the "Whaddya Think?" activity, make a photocopy of "The Bible—Can You Trust It?" handout (p. 36) for each student. If you choose the Optional Activity instead, set out paper and markers, and make enough copies of the "Pollsters!" handout (pp. 37-38) for each student.

For the Bible Connection activity, write the following Scripture references on a large sheet of newsprint: Romans 14:4-19; 1 Corinthians 6:12-20; 10:23-33; Ephesians 5:15-18; and 1 John 2:27-29. Then tape the newsprint to the wall. Set up three tables, and place each one in a different corner of your meeting room. On each table, set out newsprint, white paper, construction paper, markers, and tape. If you have other art supplies available, such as chenille wire or modeling clay, set these out on the tables as well.

Warm-Up

Whaddya Think?
(10 to 15 minutes)

As teenagers arrive, give them each a copy of "The Bible—Can You Trust It?" handout (p. 36), and have them form groups of three to six. Encourage them to read the quotes on their handouts and then discuss the questions. After seven to ten minutes, ask groups to share what they discussed. Then

ASK:

- ■ Does the Bible always tell us exactly what's right or wrong? Why or why not?
- ■ What are some examples of issues that the Bible is not crystal clear about?

SAY:

- ■ Just as there are lots of opinions *about* the Bible, Christians have different opinions about some life issues that aren't directly discussed in the Bible. <u>The Bible is your guide for life.</u> Today we're going to talk about what to do when the Bible seems unclear.

The Point ▶

* Optional Activity

(10 to 15 minutes)

Instead of doing the "Whaddya Think?" discussion, give teenagers a chance to do some of their own research about their peers' opinions regarding the Bible.

When teenagers arrive, have them form four equal groups, and distribute copies of the "Pollsters!" handouts (pp. 37-38) to each student. (A group can be as small as one person or as big as fifteen people. If you have more than sixty students, make some additional groups.) Explain that each group will be doing research by polling the entire group about a question related to the Bible. Assign one of the handout questions to each group, and then tell groups to follow the directions on their handouts to complete their research.

When they've finished, invite groups to share their charts and explain their findings.

SAY:

■ **People have a lot of different opinions about the Bible. Even in this group there are several different opinions.**

ASK:

■ **What's your reaction to our research findings?**

■ **How do you think our research results would compare to the opinions of people at your school or in our community?**

■ **If a non-Christian asked you why the Bible was important to you, what would you say?**

■ **Do you view the Bible as your guide for making life choices? Why or why not?**

The Point ▶ ■ **If <u>the Bible is your guide for life</u>, what should you do when the Bible seems unclear?**

SAY:

■ **Just as there are lots of opinions *about* the Bible, Christians have different opinions about some life issues that aren't directly discussed in the Bible. Today we're go-**

The Point ▶ **ing to look more closely at how <u>the Bible can be our guide for life</u>, even regarding issues that seem unclear.**

FYI

During the final part of the Optional activity, groups will create bar graphs to chart their findings. Some teenagers may need your help with this. Travel from group to group throughout the activity, encouraging students and answering any questions they may have.

Bible Connection

Three Shades of Gray
(20 to 25 minutes)

Have teenagers find a partner who was not in their group for the Warm-Up activity, then draw their attention to the three tables you've set up in the room. Gather all the pairs in the center of the room, and announce that you're going to give each table a name. Use one of these names for each table: "Smoking," "Taking Drugs or Drinking," and "Making Out."

Instruct pairs to go to one of the tables. (It doesn't matter which table they choose. Just make sure that the number of people at each table is approximately equal.)

SAY:

- Each of these activities is controversial to Christians. Some Christians believe that doing these things is always sinful. Others believe that doing these things is sinful only sometimes or only for some people. Today we're going to find out who's right. To begin, I'd like you and your partner to use the supplies on your table to create a giant symbol of how your assigned issue positively or negatively affects someone's life. For example, those of you at the "Smoking" table may create diseased or blackened lungs. Or those of you at the "Making Out" table may create a heart to show that making out can cause someone to feel more in love.

After two minutes, have pairs move to a different table and use the supplies there to make a giant symbol of the effects of that table's controversial issue. Then repeat the process once more so that each pair has created a giant symbol for each issue. (Have pairs keep each of their symbols with them as they travel from table to table.)

When all the pairs have finished creating their symbols, have them huddle together around one of the tables.

SAY:

- You will now attempt to solve the controversies surrounding these issues that have plagued Christians for a really long time. In order to accomplish this feat, I will provide you with several passages of Scripture that in some way relate to these "gray" areas of Christian life. You will read the Scriptures and attempt to define for Christians everywhere exactly when smoking, taking drugs or drinking, and making out become sins. Use the markers on the table to write each of your discoveries on your symbols.

Direct teenagers' attention to the verses listed on the sheet of newsprint you prepared before the study, then have pairs get started.

About five minutes into their investigations, have teenagers stop and discuss these questions with their partners:

- So far, do the two of you agree about what makes something right or wrong? Why or why not?
- How is your partner's perspective helping you work through these issues?
- <u>How is the Bible a guide for your life</u>, even when it comes to ◀ **The Point** these "gray" areas of Scripture?

After their discussions, have pairs continue their investigations.

 As pairs explore the Scriptures, they may want to apply one all-inclusive guideline to all of the controversial issues they're addressing. Don't let them. Instead, encourage them to create separate guidelines for each controversial issue. For example, in a dating relationship, where's the biblical "line" that divides physical affection from sexual sin? Or how should a Christian define drunkenness? One beer? Five beers? No beer?

Doing this will help teenagers wrestle with each of the issues more directly.

Gray Fusion
(15 to 20 minutes)

Life Application

When all the pairs have finished their investigations, have each pair use its giant symbols to present its findings to the rest of the group. Point out any trends of agreement among the group members as well as any points of disagreement.

Set out tape and string. Then

SAY:

- Now we're going to get really creative. I want you and your partner to fuse your three symbols together into a totally unique sculpture. You can use only tape and string to make your creations. Ready? Go.

Because this study encourages teenagers to wrestle with gray areas of Scripture, try to keep your own feelings about these issues secret until the end of the study—after teenagers have had the chance to work through the issues themselves. Then, if you'd like, take a few moments to tell group members what *you* believe about gray areas such as smoking, drinking, taking drugs, or making out.

By keeping quiet on your own opinions for a while, you'll essentially "force" young teenagers to grapple with the truth of the Bible on their own and will prepare them for tough situations they'll inevitably face later in life when you won't be around to teach them what's right.

When pairs have finished creating their sculptures, have them take turns presenting their creations to the rest of the group. Point out as many unique qualities of each sculpture as you can find. Then have pairs discuss these questions:

■ Were you surprised that all the sculptures looked so different, even though they all contained the same basic symbols? Why or why not?
■ Do you think one of these sculptures is more "right" than another? Why or why not?
■ How is the uniqueness of each sculpture like the uniqueness of our perspectives on these controversial issues?
■ Is it good for there to be gray areas of Scripture? Why or why not?

The Point ▶ ■ How can you let <u>the Bible be your guide for life</u>, even in the gray areas?

Ask pairs to close their discussions by praying for one another—that God would use the Bible to guide them through the gray areas in life.

The Bible—Can You Trust It?

As you are no doubt aware, not everyone has the same opinion about the Bible. Consider these quotes:

> **"A thorough knowledge of the Bible is worth more than a college education."**
> *—Theodore Roosevelt, U.S. president*

> *"The Bible and the Church have been the greatest stumbling blocks in the way of women's emancipation."*
> *—Elizabeth Cady Stanton, nineteenth century women's rights advocate*

> "I will provide a show where I balance my songs with a wholesome Bible reading. This way, fans will not only hear my so-called 'violent' point of view, but we can also examine the virtues of wonderful 'Christian' stories of disease, murder, adultery, suicide, and child sacrifice."
> *—Marilyn Manson, entertainer*

> "The Bible is good enough for me, just the old book under which I was brought up. I do not want notes or criticism, or explanations about authorship or origins, or even cross-references. I do not need, or understand them, and they confuse me."
> —Grover Cleveland, U.S. president

> *"The Bible has real significance. When I say the Bible is true, I'm saying it explains life in a way that is beyond question. The Bible says something profound about human experience."*
> *—Gary Burge, college professor*

> *"The Bible has noble poetry in it; and some clever fables; and some blood-drenched history; and a wealth of obscenity; and upwards of a thousand lies."*
> *—Mark Twain, author*

You get the gist. Now talk among yourselves:

- What's your reaction to these quotes?
- Which quote do you think comes closest to representing the most common opinion of people in your school or community? Explain.
- Which quote most closely represents the least common opinion in your school or community?
- If a non-Christian asked you why the Bible was important to you, what would you say?
- Do you view the Bible as your guide for making life choices? Why or why not?
- If the Bible is your guide for life, what should you do when the Bible seems unclear?

Pollsters

Determine your question.

Circle the question your leader assigns to your group.

1

The Bible is 100% accurate. It has no mistakes or errors.

A. I totally agree because I've read all of it (or most if it).

B. I agree because that is what I've been taught and I've read parts of it.

C. I'm not sure what I think. It does seem like it could have some mistakes in it.

D. I disagree. The Bible has several mistakes in it.

2

When it comes to making tough choices about life issues,

A. I always go to the Bible first. I make my decisions based on what I read.

B. I usually talk to my parents or friends and combine that with what I learn from the Bible and at church.

C. I talk to family members or friends. I would use the Bible, but I usually don't know where to look to find answers for the specific issues I'm facing.

D. I usually don't get advice from others or the Bible. I just do what I think is right.

3

The Bible is not the only book that contains truth about God. Books from other religions also contain the truth.

A. I agree. The Bible is a good book, but books from other religions also point people to God.

B. I'm not sure. I believe in the Bible, but I don't know if we should assume that books from other religions are wrong.

C. I disagree because I've been taught that the Bible is the only source of truth about God.

D. I disagree. I've studied both the Bible and other religions, and I believe only the Bible can direct people to the true God.

4

How do you feel about studying the Bible on your own?

A. When I study the Bible, I usually have a hard time trying to find verses that apply directly to my life.

B. I read the Bible on my own several times a week and find it very helpful.

C. I want to study the Bible on my own more, but I don't know where to start.

D. I like learning about the Bible from a teacher or pastor. I usually get bored when I try to read it on my own.

Pollsters

Do your research.

Find out what everybody thinks about your question by sending representatives to each of the other groups and recording below the answers everybody chooses. Make sure your group gets an opinion from *everybody*—including those in your own group and the representatives from other groups who are going around asking questions. As you poll one another, encourage respondents to answer honestly and to pick the letter that most closely represents what they think.

Question_____

Answer A	Answer B	Answer C	Answer D
Total:	Total:	Total:	Total:

Now chart it.

Total the number of answers for each letter. Next grab some markers and paper, and work with your group to create a chart similar to the sample to the right. Write numbers along the left-hand side of your chart, starting with zero. Choose intervals that will match your group size. (For example, if you've polled ten students, write, 0, 2, 4, 6, 8, 10. If you've polled thirty students, you'll want to write, 0, 5, 10, 15, 20, 25, 30.) Once you've got those numbers written down, work with your group to draw a bar for each letter, showing how many students chose each answer. (If you need help with this, ask your leader.)

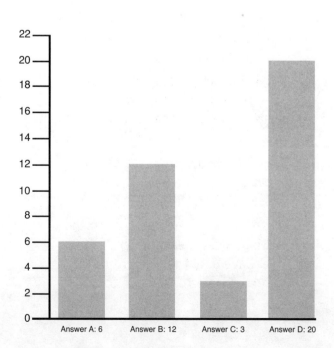

Power Potential

"Life stinks!"

You hear that phrase coming from your junior highers, and your heart aches because you know that in many ways it's true. Teenagers endure their parents' divorces. Their friends move away. They face violence at school. And they have no power to change any of it.

What teenagers need is superhuman power—you know, the ability to instantaneously transform into a superhero who can single-handedly change the world. But that's impossible.

Yet your teenagers *can* hold superhuman power in their hands if they really want to.

How? Grab a Bible.

This study explores the power of God's Word to help teenagers realize their God-given potential.

THE WORD

THE WORLD

The Point

▶God's Word has the power to change you.

Scripture Source

Psalm 119:9-16, 105;
Galatians 3:22-24;
Ephesians 5:25-27

These passages explain how Scripture can change people's lives.

James 1:21-25

James encourages Christians to hear and obey God's Word.

1 Peter 1:23-25

Peter explains how Christians can gain new life through Scripture.

THE WORD

THE WORLD

The Study at a Glance

Warm-Up (up to 10 minutes)

The Face of Change

What students will do: Draw symbols of what they want to change about themselves.

Needs: ❑ full-length mirror(s)
❑ dry-erase markers

Bonus Activity (5-10 minutes)

What students will do: Copy a picture from memory.

Needs: ❑ pencils
❑ paper
❑ drawing of shapes

Bible Connection (20-25 minutes)

Transformation

What students will do: Mirror one another's motions and study how God's Word can change their lives.

Needs: ❑ Bibles
❑ newsprint
❑ markers
❑ tape

Life Application (15-25 minutes)

Looking in the Mirror

What students will do: Search for verses that can help them change.

Needs: ❑ Bibles
❑ full-length mirror(s)
❑ dry-erase markers
❑ felt erasers or rags
❑ concordances
❑ index cards
❑ pens or pencils

Before the Study →

Find or borrow some full-length mirrors. You'll need one mirror for every ten to twelve students. (If you aren't able to find mirrors, you can use glass windows in your meeting room for this activity instead.) Also gather several felt erasers or clean rags and enough dry-erase markers so that each student has one. Set out mirrors by laying them flat on the floor.

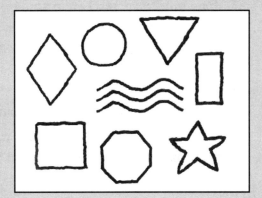

If you choose to do the Bonus Activity, draw ten shapes such as triangles, circles, and wavy lines on 8½ x 11-inch paper. (See illustration.)

Warm-Up

The Face of Change
(up to 10 minutes)

Begin by inviting students to gather around a full-length mirror and look closely at themselves.

SAY:

■ **Today we're going to discuss changing things about ourselves. If you could change one thing about yourself, what would it be? Don't say it out loud. Just think about it.** (Pause.) **Now if you thought of something physical, such as changing your hair or your height, think again. Think of something about your character or personality you'd like to change. For example, do you want to be a better listener? Do you want to be more courageous? Silently narrow it down to one thing about yourself that you'd like to change.**

Give each student a dry-erase marker, and

SAY:

■ **Think of a symbol that represents what you'd like to change, and draw it on the mirror.**

If students need help thinking of symbols, encourage them to draw a letter or a simple shape.

FYI If you don't have mirrors, have teenagers gather around windows instead and write directly on the glass with their dry-erase markers.

After teenagers have drawn their symbols, have them form foursomes to discuss these questions:

- What change does your symbol represent?
- Why do you want to change that part of you?
- Have you tried to change this part of yourself? How?
- How do you know whether you really should change that part of yourself?

SAY:

- Sometimes we wish we could change ourselves. Today we'll explore how <u>God's Word has the power to change you.</u> Before we ◀ **The Point** dive into our study, let's ask God to teach us about his Word.

PRAY:

- Dear God, thank you for loving us and giving us your Word. Please help us understand how your Word has the power to change us. Amen.

* Bonus Activity *

(5 to 10 minutes)

If you have time, try this activity after "The Face of Change" activity.

SAY:

- Let's try a quick experiment that will help us understand how we can change by studying the Bible.

Give each student paper and a pencil.

SAY:

- I'm going to show you a picture for five seconds. After I show you the picture, copy it to the best of your ability. Briefly show the group the drawing of the different shapes you made before the study, then give students sixty seconds to re-create it on their own papers.
- I'm going to show you the picture again, and as I do, compare your drawing to it. If you need to, fix your drawing so it looks just like the picture.

After two minutes, have teenagers form foursomes to discuss these questions:

- How did you feel when you first tried to re-create the picture I showed you?
- How did you feel as you tried to re-create the picture while looking at it a second time?

- Which part of the activity was easier for you? Why?
- How is looking at the picture like "looking" at God's Word and doing what it says?

SAY:

- When you saw the original picture again, you had the power to change your drawing to look more like it. In the next activity, you'll explore Scriptures that will show you how <u>God's Word has the power to change you.</u>

The Point ▶

Bible Connection

Transformation
(20 to 25 minutes)

SAY:

- Now let's explore God's Word to discover how it can change us.

Have teenagers form two groups. Assign one group James 1:21-25 and the other group 1 Peter 1:23-25.

SAY:

- In your group, read the passage I assigned to you. Then create motions that express the passage. For example, if your passage talks about reading the Bible, you could put your hands together and then open them up as if opening a book.

Give groups five minutes to read their Scriptures and create motions. When groups have finished, have each student find a partner from the other group.

SAY:

- Face your partner. I'm going to read aloud both Scripture passages, starting with the James passage. If you're from the group that created motions to James 1:21-25, do your motions while I read the verses. If you're from the other group, mirror your partner's motions. For example, if your partner raises his or her left arm, you'll raise your right arm.

Model this activity for your teenagers by having one student face you and mirror you as you raise your left arm.

Then slowly and clearly read aloud James 1:21-25 and 1 Peter 1:23-25. After reading both passages, have each pair find another pair, and have these new foursomes discuss the following questions:

- **What did you learn about the Bible as you mirrored your partner's actions?**
- **How is mirroring your partner like studying the Bible?**
- **According to the passages we read, how does studying the Bible help us change?**

SAY:

- <u>**God's Word has the power to change you.**</u> **Just as you look into a mirror to figure out what you need to change about your appearance, you can study the Bible to figure out what you need to change about your attitudes and actions. You have the power then, through God's Word, to become the person God wants you to be.**

◀ **The Point**

Tell students that they're now going to have a chance to study specific Bible passages about ways God changes people through his Word. Have foursomes read Psalm 119:9-11, 105; Galatians 3:22-24; and Ephesians 5:25-27.

As foursomes read the passages, tape newsprint to one of your walls, covering as much of the wall as you can. Then

ASK:

- **What changes did you discover that result from reading and knowing God's Word?**

Write teenagers' answers in random places on the newsprint. Make sure each foursome gives at least one answer. Then

SAY:

- **In your foursome, brainstorm some ways the Bible could change you today as it changed people in the passages you read. For example, you could suggest that to keep from sinning, you could memorize a verse that encourages you to obey God.**

After some time of study and brainstorming, explain that each foursome should choose just one of its ideas and should send a representative to write the idea on the newsprint. Explain that representatives can write no more than three words, so foursomes should try to pick an easy way to describe their ideas. Then have foursomes explain to the rest of the group what their words represent.

Have foursomes look at the banner they've worked to create together and then discuss these questions:

FYI

As teenagers discuss questions in their foursomes, see if you can join in as a listener in some of the conversations. Listen to the obstacles they mention that keep them from studying God's Word daily. Then help teenagers think of practical ways they can overcome those obstacles to make Bible reading a daily habit.

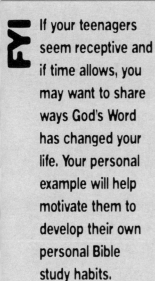

FYI

If your teenagers seem receptive and if time allows, you may want to share ways God's Word has changed your life. Your personal example will help motivate them to develop their own personal Bible study habits.

■ Which words or phrases on the banner draw your attention? Why?

■ What do you think of the banner we created together? Would you like to change anything about it? If so, what would you like to change and why?

■ Do you think you're a finished product? Why or why not?

■ What's one way God's Word could change you?

■ What keeps you from reading God's Word each day?

■ Based on our Bible exploration, will you change your Bible-reading habits? Why or why not?

SAY: _____

■ <u>God's Word has the power to change you.</u> As you study ◀ **The Point** God's Word daily, God can use it to make you into the person he created you to be.

Life Application # Looking in the Mirror
(15 to 25 minutes)

SAY: _____

The Point ▶ ■ <u>God's Word has the power to change you.</u> But the Bible can change you only when you read it to discover what you need to change about yourself and how to change it.

Have students gather around the mirror or window they wrote on during the Warm-Up activity.

SAY: _____

■ Each of you has created a symbol of something you'd like to change in your life. In your foursome, use a concordance to find Bible verses that address the change you want to make. For example, if you want to become a better listener, you might find James 1:19 a helpful passage.

Give each foursome a concordance, and explain how to use it.
As foursomes are looking up their verses, give each student a dry-erase marker, a felt eraser or rag, an index card, and a pen or pencil.

SAY: _____

■ When you find a passage that will help you change, erase the symbol you drew, and write the reference to the Bible passage you found in its place.

Encourage students to also write the verse they found on an index card that they can take home and use in their personal Bible study.

When all the students have finished writing, have them crack open their Bibles one more time and turn to Psalm 119:9-16. Encourage them to read the verses silently and think about the importance of making the Bible a top priority in their lives. Once they've all read these verses, invite several volunteers to read them aloud as a closing prayer while the other students read along.

FYI

To help your students really dive into Bible study, check out the Forty-Day Bible Study Challenge described on page 47. Issue this challenge to your students, and see how their lives are changed as a result of God's Word!

Changed 4 Life

Wrap up your study on *Understanding the Bible* by giving your students this Forty-Day Bible Study Challenge. Invite them to commit to read nine Bible verses a day for the next forty days. At this rate, they'll read all of Psalm 119 twice. Encourage students to keep a notebook so each day after they read they can write their answers to this question: How does this apply to my life?

At the end of the forty days, encourage students to look over their notebooks and read all the comments they made. Celebrate the students' efforts by inviting them over for pizza. While you meet together, invite them to share how this study has changed their lives. Use some of these questions to guide your discussion:

- How has this experience changed your perspective of God's Word?
- How has this experience changed you personally?
- How will you continue this Bible study habit now that the Forty-Day Bible Study Challenge is over?

Look for the Whole Family of *Faith 4 LiFE* Bible Studies!

Senior High Books
- **Family Matters**
- **Is There Life After High School?**
- **Prayer**
- **Sharing Your Faith**

Junior High Books
- **Becoming a Christian**
- **Finding Your Identity**
- **God's Purpose for Me**
- **Understanding the Bible**

Preteen Books
- **Being Responsible**
- **Getting Along With Others**
- **God in My Life**
- **Going Through Tough Times**

Coming Soon!

for Senior High
- *Applying God's Word*
- *Christian Character*
- *Sexuality*
- *Your Christian ID*
- *Believing in Jesus*
- *Following Jesus*
- *Worshipping 24/7*
- *Your Relationships*

for Junior High
- *Choosing Wisely*
- *Friends*
- *My Family Life*
- *Sharing Jesus*
- *Fighting Temptation*
- *How to Pray*
- *My Life as a Christian*
- *Who Is God?*

for Preteens
- *Building Friendships*
- *How to Make Great Choices*
- *Succeeding in School*
- *What's a Christian?*
- *Handling Conflict*
- *Peer Pressure*
- *The Bible and Me*
- *Why God Made Me*

Visit your local Christian bookstore,
or contact Group Publishing, Inc., at 800-447-1070.
www.grouppublishing.com